Mind Shifts

Catch the Wave of Your Greater Self!

Also by Jan Gault

BOOKS

5 Minutes A Day Dream-Action Path
The Mighty Power of Your Beliefs
Motivational Messages for Miracle Moments
Quotes, Questions & Actions for Global Understanding
Play Your Way to Prosperity
Free Time: Making Your Leisure Count

AUDIO/CD PROGRAMS

Perseverance & Passion
Strategies for Success
25 Ways to Build Self-Esteem & Success
The Principle of Purpose
Vision & Courage
Prosperity Principles & Beliefs
Also Available: Inspirational/Motivational Podcasts

Bulk Purchase Discounts

Books are available at deep quantity discounts with bulk purchase for business, educational, or sales promotional use. For information, please e-mail ocean@drjan.net.

For information on Jan's seminars, training programs, books, and other products, please contact:

Jan Gault International™
415-367-3513 prosper@drjan.net
http://www.drjan.net

Online Audio/Video Consultations with Dr. Jan Are Currently Available

Mind Shifts

Catch the Wave of Your Greater Self!

Jan Gault, Ph.D.

http://www.drjan.net

Ocean Manor

Publishers Cataloging in Publication Data

Gault, Jan L.

Mind shifts : catch the wave of your greater self / Jan Gault. —
Kailua-Kona, Hawaii : Ocean Manor, ©2011.

p. ; cm.

ISBN: 978-0-923699-42-0 (pbk.) ; 0923699-42-2 (pbk.)
Includes bibliographical references.

1. Self-help techniques. 2. Self-realization. 3. Self-actualization (Psychology) 4. Achievement motivation. 5. Success—Psychological aspects. 6. Happiness—Psychological aspects. 7. Personal coaching. I. Title.

BF632 .G384 2011 2011916889
158/.1—dc23 1201

Library of Congress Control Number: 2011916889

Manufactured in the United States of America
10 9 8 7 6 5 4 3 2 1

This edition is printed on acid-free paper that meets all ANSI standards for archival quality paper.

Disclaimer

Neither author Jan Gault nor the publisher assumes responsibility or liability arising from the use of any information contained in this book. Under no circumstances shall Jan Gault, Jan Gault International™, or Ocean Manor be liable for any direct, indirect, punitive, incidental, special, or consequential damages arising out of or in any way connected with the use of *Mind Shifts: Catch the Wave of Your Greater Self.*

Cover Design by Deborah Perdue, Illumination Graphics
Cover Image by Noel Powell | Dreamstime.com
Book Interior Layout by Deborah Perdue, Illumination Graphics
Copy Editing by Kathy K. Grow, DoWriteEditing

Dedication

This book is dedicated to each of my readers seeking their authentic rhythm of being.

I also dedicate it to my brother Rich.

Contents

Introduction

Catching the wave of yourself—i.e., your heart, your true self, who you were meant to be—will only come when you are ready, and open to change. Though with us always, we miss it as we get caught up in the melodrama of our lives. The wave of you is your deepest self and your highest self . . . your highest vibration and what you continually move toward . . . the emergent self, seeking to co-create. Just as you consciously reach to possess it, it eludes your grasp, gently telling you there is no need to hold on. It is simply there.

Transformation is continually taking place. The wave is there; it's just not there to grasp or hold on to. Instead, it's there to ride and to lift you to new and amazing levels of being. And, as you catch the wave and your new self begins to unfold, an expansive new world appears, and reappears.

Staying within its mighty presence and power is what this book is about. Although we touch its presence daily—perhaps at the sight of a beautiful sunset, a flower blossom, or a baby's smile—old triggers snap us right back into our conditioned self that gets discouraged, sad, and upset. We recognize this as it's happening, but, once incited, our minds are off and running down the same unproductive paths. How do you stop it in its tracks and get back to who you really are?

Just how do you deal with the misbehaving mind-prattle keeping you from the natural joy of creative living? Is there some way to retain the calm presence of those magic moments? To have the freedom of thought that keeps you out of all the mind-pits threatening your happiness and your vision for a better life?

Do you need a full-blown spiritual transformation to knock you loose from the old mind habits and bring on a new perception and rhythm of being?

You, like many, may have had just such a spiritual transformation at some point in your life. And, for a time, you looked at the world with new eyes. Everything did indeed look quite different. Suddenly you were a new person inhabiting a new world. No doubt about it.

As time went by, though, the mind got to buzzing again, and you strayed farther and farther away from that world. Now, only the occasional moment of wonder dances across your life.

So you read and journal and attend workshops. You participate in teleconferences and social media forums. You search for the magic and peace and wisdom.

Changing Your Mind

Anyone who has attempted to change their mind habits is well aware of how daunting it can be.

Yes, most of us are now mind-emotion-action literate. We understand how our beliefs, thinking habits, and thoughts trigger emotions and actions. And we know that many of our mind's ingrained thought-emotion tracks are limiting our power and happiness. Most of us are also well educated on "good thinking habits"—the ones that work in our favor and move us in the directions we desire.

We have the knowledge, but have never learned the solid remedial routines to shift permanently our mind's content in new directions.

The first time one of the old triggers comes our way, then annoyance, anger, discouragement, or frustration sets in. Instead of consciously stepping free from their grip, we fall into a struggle mode mired in our past toxic habits.

How can we get it, then? How can we own this illusive consciousness that flutters in and out of our lives, but never quite lands to stay?

Is there some sort of mind exercise we can perform to rid ourselves of the old dysfunctional ways? Permanently lift us out of the funks we fall into? Are there procedures we can take to shift our thoughts and thinking enduringly along the lines that will keep us focused on our visions? That will once and for all let us attract what we truly desire, and reap more moments of wonder, joy, and fulfillment? Are there strategies that can let us soar in that great universal state beckoning us?

Yes.

I will be revealing many of these here, and offering you the vital sessions to put them in place. You will also learn a variety of powerful perception and perspective processes. Each will help you ride the wave of your authentic self more consistently.

This book is about shifting to a new level of being, catching the wave to transform consistently your life and become a co-creator with the Universe. It is about embracing where you are now and then lifting yourself beyond the confines of the ordinary to the extraordinary.

This does not mean that you're going to exist in some mindless, blissed-out, inactive state. It means instead that you will no longer be simply surviving out of your conditioned self, but choosing and acting out of your inspirational sphere. Your greater self will be at the helm, orchestrating your life.

Believe deep down in your heart
that you're destined to do great things.
~Joe Paterno

I

Your Wave Style: Exploring Your Patterns

The secret of success is to be in harmony
with existence, to be always calm,
to let each wave of life wash us
a little farther up the shore.
~Cyril Connolly

CHAPTER 1

Your Wave Style

He who knows others is wise. He who knows himself is enlightened.
~Lao Tzu

Know thyself, and thou shalt know the universe.
~Socrates

Getting to Know Yourself

One of the wisest pronouncements ever made may well be to "Know Thyself." Though frequently quoted, my experience with clients and students has been that few of us, even in our later years, know much about ourselves, or the mysterious black box that governs our behaviors. This section is to help you better understand just who you are, your vision, your passion, and what some of your limitations might be. This in turn will serve as a foundation for targeting the strategies ahead best suited to your particular wave style.

Everyone has a distinct wave pattern. Learning a little more about your unique pattern will point you in the direction of how to begin catching the wave, and realizing your dreams for a more meaningful life.

In this chapter, we will especially be exploring your "freedom moments." What do you do when you're most free to be yourself?

How you spend your time when you're freest to be yourself gets at the heart of who you are and how you will fare. Whether you spend the bulk of your discretionary time watching mindless television shows or fulfilling your deepest desires speaks volumes about who you are, and your destiny.

Your wave style is intimately tied to your big dream in life and your vision for a better life. The activities below will help you highlight your core desires and dominant thinking patterns as a starting point to understanding.

Consider the questions below, following through with the activities for each. I encourage you to do this before going to the next chapter. It will be time well spent! In the process, you will discover your unique wave style and how it is impacting your life.

Where You Are Now: Your Starting Point

Thinking

What do you think about most frequently? What thoughts and images continually invade your mind?

Activity: For the next twenty-four hours, make a note of your recurring thoughts. What percentage of these thoughts would you say are in accord with your highest self and the life you'd like to live—10%, 25%, 70%? Guesstimate a number and write it down.

Feeling

Do you have a dominant feeling that permeates your life? What is it?

Activity: Write down the first emotion that comes to mind for this question. Why do you suppose this is so? Is this the way you like to feel?

Being

Are you generally focused within the present moment, or does your mind wander off into worry over past mistakes and future concerns?

Activity: See if you can identify a focal point in your life. Is this where you want to be?

One Word

Consider one word that best describes what you're about. For example, Oprah has said that the word "love" best describes who she is. For you, might it be "kind," "adventurous," "optimistic"? Or, conversely, maybe it's "tired," "unhappy," "bored"?

Activity: If you get stuck in coming up with a word, try the following exercise:

> Complete the sentence "I am . . ." ten times, quickly saying whatever pops into your head. Then select the one word from these that best describes you.

Time/Action

How are you arranging the minutes and hours of your days, weeks, months, years? What takes up the bulk of your time? Be honest! Is this in sync with who you are or want to become? Are you arranging your time in harmony with what you truly yearn for in life?

Activity: Spend a few minutes considering the above questions.

There is never a better measure of what a person is than what he does when he's absolutely free to choose.

~Bern Williams

Your Heart's Desires

Your Dream Vacation

- If you had one month off work and money was not an issue, what would you be doing?
- Where would you go? Hawaii, the Amazon, Asia, Europe? Or would you stay at home?

- What time of year would you take your vacation? Summer, autumn, winter, spring?
- With whom would you prefer to spend this time? Family, friends, your sweetheart, new acquaintances, or just yourself?

Activity: Write a one-paragraph description of your dream vacation answering the above questions.

Playing God

- If you were God and created the Universe, what would it look like?
- What would you look like?

Activity: Bullet-point five essential features for each of the above questions.

The Love of Your Life

- What kind of things are you most curious about?
- What inspires you most?
- What truly makes your heart sing?
- What do you find positively—no questions about it—thrilling?
- What gives you the greatest sense of satisfaction?
- What do you feel is the greatest gift you have to give to yourself and the world?
- When have you experienced your happiest moments?

Activity: Don't think too hard about your answers to the above. Let them flow naturally.

Now go back through them and ask why for each. This will give you a wealth of information about yourself, where you are at this moment in time, and the direction to take in your transformation experience. Remember, transformation is always occurring. We're seeking to facilitate this process through active participation.

Finally, drawing on your responses from the above, draft a two-paragraph vision statement.

Even if you've written vision statements in the past, do this again now. In the next chapter, you'll be refining and expanding your vision statement.

Vision gives you the impulse to make the picture your own.
~Robert Collier

CHAPTER 2

Your Big Dream

Before your dreams can come true, you have to have those dreams.
~Joyce Brothers

If your dream is right for you, it will lift you beyond your current self, into the energy of your emergent being. The right dream will be powerful enough to inspire you to continue no matter how tired you are or how many other demands are encroaching on your time. And it will be strong enough to survive, no matter how many people pooh-pooh it, and no matter what crises suddenly demand your attention. No matter what!

If your dream does not rise to this litmus test, you need either to revise it or consider a new one. In other words, if your dream is on the mark, it will align with your deepest and truest self—the unique wave of you.

Ask yourself the questions below to clarify further your dream and vision. Questions are a powerful catalyst for change!

Your Big Dream

- What are the key benefits of my dream? To myself? To others?
- In what ways does my big dream evoke my passion?
- Ultimately, what difference will it make to realize my dream? For you? For others? For society? For the Universe?

- How does my dream vision align with the people in my life? My family? Friends? Colleagues?
- What larger purpose does my dream serve?
- How does my vision align with the greater good of all, i.e., your community, country, and world? (As social beings, our self-fulfillment and happiness depend in part on how well we're contributing to the collective whole.)
- Finally, is there something else I might be doing that is more powerful and inspiring to me?

Activity: After pondering these questions, refine the vision statement you drafted in the last chapter.

Where would you be? What would you be thinking about? How would you feel? What would you be doing?

See yourself and your surroundings in your mind's eye. Rewrite your vision statement, answering these questions as best you can before moving on. Do this now.

Keep your dream close to your heart by reading over your vision statement several times a day. Keeping your dream statement in front of you, along with employing the strategies ahead, will help minimize the mind-pitfalls that sap your energy and keep you trapped in your conditioned self.

Start Now

The time to begin realizing your dreams for a better life is now. You took the first step by obtaining a copy of this book. No need to wait until you've completed reading it. Begin right now to move in the direction of your heart's desires!

If you've always wanted to write a book and the words won't come, start scribbling; make up anything but stay with it for an allotted time each day.

If you're attempting to lose weight and stuck on starting to exercise, redefine it as your "fun time" and stay with it for just five minutes. Whatever you can do, do. But begin.

If you're burned out on a dead-end job, or haven't yet found your dream career, get online and type in your dream position. Revise your resumé. Check out career listings on craigslist. Just do something.

You'll find that, when you make even the tiniest move toward living the life for which you were intended, the Universe will step in to support you. And you'll be given plenty of help in the pages ahead. A myriad of tools are there to guide and assist you in fulfilling your dreams and living up to the person you were meant to be.

We begin in the next chapter by disarming and dismantling the old ways that have led you off the path of your true self.

Most people never run far enough on their first wind, to find out if they've got a second. Give your dreams all you've got, and you'll be amazed at the energy that comes out of you.

~William James

II
Disarm & Dismantle the Old

Every time you let go of something limiting,
you create space for something better.
~Stephen C. Paul

CHAPTER 3

Blast Out the Old Thinking Habits: 21 Ploys to Discharge Flawed Beliefs and Thoughts

You must weed your mind as you would weed your garden.
~Astrid Alauda

Creating a Miracle Space

Twenty-one "thought blaster" strategies are provided below. Sample them and see which ones are most effective for your personality and situation. Each is designed to release you from toxic thought-spikes that jeopardize your happiness and well-being, by lifting you "out of your thoughts" into a pause-zone where you can regroup and shift direction. From this venue, you are positioned to explore new realms of being.

I've given each a short title as a memory aid for quick recall when you need it. Practice as many of these as you can over the next twenty-four hours. This shouldn't be difficult since the majority of us typically have hundreds of negative thoughts daily. Next, highlight or make a note of at least five strategies you found most helpful to you.

A Word of Caution: Remember the little red engine. Don't get discouraged if at first you don't succeed. Persevere! Persevere! Persevere! You will prevail.

1. Tsunami Surge

Visualize a great tsunami flooding your mind and washing away negative thoughts and beliefs. Watch the giant waves cleansing your mind of afflictive thoughts: "I'll always be overweight" . . . "I'll never find a decent job" . . . "I'll always be stuck in this awful relationship". . . "I'll never find the guy of my dreams." See them all wash away and dissolve into the ocean.

2. Call Up Your Curiosity

Become curious about your mind's makeup. When you call up your curiosity about the ways in which your mind is running, you are no longer trapped by the emotional component; you are simply wondering how it came to be this way, and what is it about your mind that is evoking the anger or sadness or frustration. When you shift into a curiosity mode, you free yourself from unwelcome emotional discharges.

3. Canvas Your Thought Stream

Distract yourself from your stream of thoughts by painting a picture out of them on a canvas in your mind. See your thought stream swirling around forming circles, faces, mountains—whatever you imagine. What does it look like? What colors do you see? Notice that, when you perform this activity, any annoying thoughts lose their grip on you.

4. A Long Train

Distance yourself from vexing cognitions by visualizing a long train carrying them away farther and farther from you. See the train chugging along the tracks faster and farther away, until all the unwanted thought-baggage has been carried off.

5. Thunder

Hear and visualize a loud thunder "boom" knocking out a whole pattern of negative thoughts that's attempting to take hold of your mind.

6. In the Gutter

Create a large deep hole or gutter in your mind's eye. See it vividly. Now, whenever a negative thought crosses your mind, dump it into the hole and cover it with dirt. That's where it belongs, in the gutter.

7. Drum Boom

Break up a vicious thought stream by inserting a drumbeat at regular intervals.

For example, say you've been having the frequent thought, "I'm never going to be able to lose this weight!" Now think: "I'm (boom) never going (boom boom) to lose (boom boom boom) this weight!"

Next, take out any negative words invading the phrases in your mind (in this case, "never"), while at the same time adding the drumbeats for emphasis. Thus, "I'm (boom) going (boom boom) to lose (boom boom boom) this weight!" Repeat three times.

8. Pay Attention

Observe your mind's content—your thoughts and beliefs. What do you hear yourself saying? Can you see your thoughts? Practice disassociating yourself from the constant chain of chatter inside your head by looking at what's happening.

When you step into your observer mode, you set yourself free from your current pattern of thoughts and thinking. You are just there watching. Not thinking, not judging, not feeling. Free of the whole cognitive shebang. Free of the rampant banter weighing you down.

9. Favorite Song Shift

As negative thoughts start to rush in, consciously recall a favorite song. Hear and feel the beat of the music. Sing the lyrics silently. The rhythm and words will knock out the unwanted thoughts attempting to gain entrance.

Tip: You need to program in a favorite song ahead of time to have it quickly available in your memory repertoire.

10. Zumba Dance

Zumba dance on your recurring negative thoughts. See the words breaking up into vowels and consonants; that's all they are. They can have no power over you unless you allow them. See yourself stomping them out to the beat of the music.

11. Black Tar Balls

Visualize your negative thoughts getting stuck in round black tar balls and rolling off into the yonder. See them getting smaller and smaller until they disappear from sight.

12. Deny Entry

As rogue thoughts attempt to gain entry into your mind, bolt the door and deny them access. This ploy only works if you discern them before they grab hold of your mind. Again, this comes with practice.

13. Hurricane Drop

Picture a hurricane swirling away your toxic thoughts and dropping them deep into the ocean, never to return. Try to visualize them sinking far into the depths of the sea.

14. Shock Treatment

Tune in to some staccato music on your radio. Turn it up full blast to prevent your brain from generating negative thoughts.

This doesn't work for everyone. If you're sensitive to sound, try it with the volume lower, and visualize the rapid beats of the music pounding out the thoughts.

15. Crazy Postures

The moment an unwanted thought crosses your mind, wrap yourself into a shape like a pretzel or a doughnut. If this is uncomfortable, just visualize yourself in these postures. Visualization can be as effective as the physical act.

When you switch your thinking to your posture, the unwanted thought sequence melts away.

16. Rapid Eye Movement

Whenever an uninvited thought strikes, immediately start rolling your eyes. Look up and down. Look to the left and to the right. Continue eye rolls until the thoughts stop.

17. Humor

Recall an amusing incident. Replay it in your mind when a troublesome thought appears. Note that you'll need to have identified some amusing incidents prior to using this ploy. Our thoughts strike instantly, almost without warning. Unless your mind has been prepped ahead of time with the necessary resources, this cannot work.

18. Laugh Therapy

Laughter is good for most anything that ails you. You can train yourself to laugh on cue. Start by saying, "He he he, ha ha ha," for one minute. Feel foolish? Good! Stop taking yourself so seriously. I love this tool and use it often myself.

19. Chill Out the Toxics

Stop and exhale the toxic thoughts and feelings popping up in your mind. Take thirty seconds and breathe deeply in and out. Create a space in your mind for new empowering beliefs.

20. Flip the Circuit Breaker

Your thoughts race around in your mind, interlaced in the energy circuits created over the years. To stop stubborn thought streams, sometimes we just need to pull the circuit breaker. Visualize a master switch attached to your string of thoughts. See yourself flipping it off. This one takes a little practice but is very effective after being rehearsed a few times.

21. Pop the Bubble

Your thoughts and thinking inhabit swirls of energy bubbles in your brain. When hostile thoughts pop into your mind, picture a pin puncturing the bubbles and releasing the unwanted thoughts and emotions. This is another of my favorites!

Don't let yourself be overwhelmed by the above list. Practice and use those that feel comfortable. After a short while, they'll become second nature to you. Even if you only make regular use of one or two of the strategies, you'll find that your nuisance thought clusters won't stand a chance!

Once you've stopped the runaway villains dead in their tracks, you must fill the vacuum. You need to engage the miracle space you've just created with those thoughts and thinking habits that align with your true self, your unique wave. We begin by exploring a variety of focus tools in the next chapter.

When I let go of what I am, I become what I might be.
~The Tao Te Ching

III

Focus Focus Focus

Our thoughts create our reality—where we put our focus is the direction we tend to go.

~Peter McWilliams

CHAPTER 4

Focus Shifts to Lift You Out of a Funk: 26 Prompters to Help Keep You on the Path

You must remain focused on your journey to greatness.
~Les Brown

Focus Prompters

Focus is such a critical component of achieving your desires and dreams, I've listed twenty-six focus prompters below to help keep you on the path and attuned to your wave rhythm. Highlight the ones that resonate most with you, bookmarking them for later reference.

These are to be used in conjunction with the thought blasters in the previous chapter. The idea is first to stop the negative thoughts from firing, then quickly fill the gap by shifting your focus to mind material in tune with your greater self.

If you're like many people, as you go through the tools below, an opposite negative string of thoughts may invade your mind instead of the intended positive ones.

For example, for the first one I've listed—"Focus on what's going right"—the thought "Nothing's going right for me now!" might pop up, along with a flood of thoughts about all the problems in your life.

If this happens, don't fight it; just continue gently to shift your focus to what's going right in your life: you had a good dinner last night, you own a computer and a cell phone, you live in America and don't have to worry about security police breaking into your home and kidnapping you, you have a great daughter or son. And so on. The more you can come up with, the better. You're seeking to shatter irreversibly the old negative patterns, leaving no space whatsoever for their mischief.

Once the new wave patterns are fully mastered, there will be no room left in the chambers of your mind for menace-thoughts keeping you from your desires and dreams.

As you review each of the focus tools below, stop a moment, reflect, then give your attention to that topic until you've fully secured it in your mind. Begin now.

Note: These are not listed in any particular order of importance. Feel free to skip around to the ones that resonate most with you. I do, however, encourage you to sample as many as possible.

1. What's Going Right

Focus on what's going right in your life rather than on all the problems. You have enough food to eat. The sun is shining outside and you're breathing fresh air. Your car is running. Your parents love you.

2. What's Possible

Focus on the vision of what can be for yourself. If you like, include a vision of what you desire for your family and community. Add this to the vision statement you drafted earlier.

3. Nature's Wonders

Focus on the natural beauty and wonders of nature—flowers, trees, sky, singing birds, mountains, lakes, ocean, and waterfalls. As a nature lover, this is one of my favorite focus tools and never fails to lift my spirits.

4. The Best in Someone

Focus on the best about a person in your life, what they're doing right, and the person they could become. This is an excellent tool when you're having minor relationship issues or have to deal with a difficult co-worker. It takes a little longer to master, but the results are decidedly worthwhile.

5. Marvels of Science

Focus on the amazing technological and scientific advances that have given us so much freedom and pleasure. Despite all the shortcomings of modern science, we have much to be grateful for: airplanes that take us to see family and friends; medical discoveries that ease suffering; cell phones, computers, ebooks, videos, musical instruments, cameras, apps—a long, long list.

6. A Special Achievement

Focus on a special triumph you've had in the last week or year. This needn't be anything big. Maybe you faced up to a fear, started a new project you'd been procrastinating about, learned a helpful insight, or didn't react in kind to a hurtful remark. Bask in the glow of that triumph.

7. Thought Mantra

Focus on a new mantra to replace an unhappy thought sequence that keeps running through your mind. I use Dr. Suess's, "Life is good, life is fun, tomorrow is another one." Granted, it's not always easy to shift consciously to the good in life when your situation is bleak. A more neutral mantra you might try is, "I will persist until I succeed."

8. Inspirational Message

Focus on an inspirational message—an encouraging quotation or short poem. For example, consider, "My greatness lies in becoming myself."

9. Power of Choice

Focus on your amazing power to choose your own thoughts, dreams, and actions. Think about this. What a power!

10. Physical Pleasures

Focus on one of the physical pleasures you can enjoy on earth—a massage, a hug, a touch, an orgasm. Recreate it in your mind.

11. Wonders of the Universe

Focus on the miraculous wonders of the Universe—the planets, stars, moon, and sun. Gazing up on a star-filled sky, you'll find it impossible not to marvel at such a miracle.

12. Your Amazing Human Body

Focus on your amazing human body and all it can do—a brain to plan and think, a heart that beats for living, a voice for song, lungs for breathing, feet for dancing, ...

13. Power of Mind and Spirit

Focus on your incredible awareness of our power of mind and spirit. What would we be without our extraordinary awareness? And most of us use but a tiny sliver of our potential awareness. As your transformation process accelerates, your awareness and power will mushroom beyond your wildest dreams!

14. Fascinating Sounds

Focus on all the sounds we as humans can hear and enjoy: a cascading waterfall, the patter of raindrops, a cat's purr, a friend's comforting words, a baby's sigh.

15. Great Masters of Old

Focus on one of the great masters of the past who has changed our world through her or his ideas and influence. This might be a favorite author, a scientist, or a humanitarian.

16. Schools Educating Our Youth

Focus on all the schools that have been built to better educate our youth. Did you know there are over one hundred million elementary schools in the world? Yes, many need improvement—and there are countless dedicated individuals working toward this goal.

17. Your Imagination

Focus on your amazing powers of imagination to dream, and to act in the direction of your dream. Einstein once said, "Imagination is more powerful than knowledge."

18. Your Senses

Focus on each of your senses—hearing, speaking, smelling, seeing, touching—and all they make possible for you. Could all this really have been just an accident of the Universe?

19. Beauty

Focus on beauty wherever you find it. In spite of the difficult challenges in our lives and the world, we can usually find a glimmer of hope and beauty when we seek it out. Focusing on the beauty in the world is not a denial of the ills that face us, but a place to renew our wisdom and regain our strength. Vincent Van Gogh said, "If you truly love Nature, you will find beauty everywhere."

20. A Special Person

Focus on someone you've known who has given kindness and service to others. Watching videos of Humanitarian Hero awards is always uplifting. Closer to home might be a member of your community who has assisted a person in need.

21. An Insight

Focus on a valuable learning experience or insight that you've had. One of my most thrilling insights was when I realized I could choose the content of my mind according to the consequences I desired.

22. Undiscovered Worlds

Focus on all the unknowns yet to be discovered—the meanings of your dreams, new planets and peoples, ...

23. An Act of Kindness

Focus on an act of kindness you have experienced. Often we get so caught up in all the inconsiderate actions of others, we forget about the many kindnesses we've received, e.g., a hug from a friend when you were feeling down, a special birthday gift, a tender caress.

24. Alive

Focus on why you're happy to be alive. On a down day, you certainly may feel there's nothing at all to be happy about. Don't force this, but gently nudge your thinking toward exploring why life is good and you're here, a person alive in a Universe of remarkable dimensions.

25. Made You Smile

Focus on something that made you laugh or smile this week (another one of my favorites, and easy to master). Keep by your desk a memory cue card of an incident that sparked a smile or laughter. A cartoon or picture is perfect also. The idea is to have something handy when your thoughts take a downturn.

26. You in Six Months

Focus on the person you'd like to be in six months. Give some extra thought to this one. Just how would you like to be thinking, feeling, and living? How would your life change?

Before moving on to the next chapter, review the focus prompters above again and express your appreciation for the many things for which you're grateful.

When I first started creating this list, I was feeling frustrated about an overload of responsibilities in my life. However, by the time I'd finished, my mood had shifted to a deep appreciation for the many gifts and special blessings in my own life. I hope this will be the case for you as well.

You can't depend on your judgment when your imagination is out of focus.
~Mark Twain

IV
Power Up with the New

You are a living magnet. What you attract into your life is in harmony with your dominant thoughts.
~Brian Tracy

CHAPTER 5

Belief Lineup: Targeting an Area for Change

Nurture your mind with great thoughts, for you will never go any higher than you think.

~Benjamin Disraeli

Getting Specific

All right, now you've learned how to break up and clear out the old. You've discovered how to create a miracle space in your mind to allow for the new. And you've learned to apply some focus shift tools when you're feeling down and out.

The next step is to decide on an area of your life in which you'd especially like to see some improvement.

Consider your priorities at this time in your life. Maybe you've going through some tough economic times and desperately need to improve your financial situation. Or you're experiencing some challenging relationship issues. Is getting out of a bad relationship or cultivating a new relationship your main concern right now? How's your fitness and weight program going? Just stepped on your bathroom scale and shrieked?

While you may have several areas in which you'd like to see improvement, I want you to start with only one aspect of your life.

Mastering one area will facilitate creating change along other dimensions later. If you're unsure where to begin, use the short Priority Scale Meter provided below.

Priority Scale Meter

This is a scale designed to help you determine what's most important to you at this point in time, and where you'd like to begin making changes.

Rank each of the following dimensions on a scale from 1 to 7, with 7 being the highest. For example, if "Wealth/Fiscal Fitness" is of primary importance to you, you would place a 7 beside this dimension. Conversely, if your "Relationships" are going well and are of little concern to you at this time, you would place a 1 beside this dimension. This is a forced choice questionnaire. You must use a different number for each category. It's likely you'll be tempted to assign the same number to more than one category. Don't! ***Use each number only once!***

_____ Wealth/Fiscal Fitness (financial security, freedom from financial worries, investments, . . .)

_____ Education (continued learning, reading, attending conferences and workshops, . . .)

_____ Relationships (family, friends, romance, cultivating new relationships, . . .)

_____ Health/Fitness (nutrition, slimming down, aerobics, dance, . . .)

_____ Service to Others (helping those in need, making a difference, volunteer work, . . .)

_____ Leisure/Fun & Enjoyment (vacation, traveling, social activities, . . .)

_____ Career (finding a rewarding career path, having meaningful work, . . .)

Note: if you're reading this as an ebook, use the note function or a separate piece of paper to assign the numbers. Do this now.

Line Up the New Beliefs and Thoughts in Your Mind

Below are seven belief clusters, one for each of the vital dimensions of your life. Highlight the one you've targeted to begin your path to change. If the affirmations do not ring true for you now, think of them as real possibilities that will unfold in your life with practice.

Important! It's not enough simply to repeat the belief clusters. Mindless repetition without the emotional glue, imagery, rhythm, and physical reinforcement will get you nowhere! You need to own the new belief structures by making use of the imprinting strategies offered in the next chapters. That is, they must become your own authentic internal dialogue and how you think, feel, and act.

Belief Clusters

Wealth/Fiscal Fitness

- I embrace the challenges in my life.
- I create opportunities in my life.
- I give myself permission to do what I love.
- I am true to my personal vision of prosperity.
- I deserve prosperity and financial well-being.

Education

- I view life as a learning experience.
- I enjoy learning new things.
- I believe in lifelong learning.
- I keep an open mind when confronted with new ideas.
- I view mistakes as growth experiences.

Relationships

- I am moving toward a better relationship.
- I am treated with kindness and respect by my partner.
- I deserve to be treated well.
- I am in a relationship that affirms my self-worth.
- I deserve a good relationship.

Health/Fitness

- I eat those foods that are good for me and the planet.
- I have a regular physical activity routine that is fun.
- I am at the optimal weight for my height and frame.
- I enjoy staying healthy.
- I treat my body with the respect it deserves.

Service to Others

- I believe I am here to make a contribution to humanity, no matter how small.
- I believe in making a positive difference in the lives of others.
- I act with honesty and integrity in my dealings with others.
- I assume personal responsibility for helping those in need.
- I set a good example for others, and do not waste energy worrying about their choices and actions.

Leisure/Fun & Enjoyment

- I reward myself for my successes, however small they may seem.
- I take charge of my free moments without feeling guilty.
- I choose my activities.
- I arrange my free time as I choose—to nap, participate in fun activities, or creative acts toward my goals and dreams.
- I celebrate my life.

Career

- I have consciously chosen my career path.

- I am in a career that is fulfilling.
- I enjoy my work.
- I find meaning in doing what is necessary.
- I deserve a career that is rewarding.

Each of the above clusters targets specific areas in which you may seek improvement. Master one category before going on to your next area of improvement.

In addition, you will want to memorize (yes, memorize!) and regularly affirm the five ***core beliefs of empowerment*** listed below.

I know I've been asking a lot of you in the activities in this book. I wish I could tell you that simply reading through the book would change your life. It won't. You need to step up to the challenge, trust in yourself and the Universe, and consistently follow through. The time you spend will be well worth it!

After all, think about the years and years you've spent in grade school, high school, and college, studying for exams and "getting educated." The time required here pales in comparison. And it's for your own enrichment and happiness. The Universe is there waiting to shower you with its abundance.

Core Beliefs of Empowerment

- I believe in the power to improve my life.
- I believe in the Universe and my emergent self.
- I believe in myself, my capabilities, and my service or product.
- I believe my efforts are making a difference even when I see no tangible results.
- I believe I deserve success and happiness.

After committing the above core beliefs of empowerment to memory, go to the next chapter to begin learning powerful strategies for making the new beliefs and thought clusters your own. Once you fully own the new beliefs, your vibration will spiral and a vibrant new life unfold for you.

In the pages ahead you will be introduced to five simple steps, along with a variety of cognitive, emotive, rhythmic, and physical tools. At the foundation of all these are spiritual shift processes. A special section summarizes these key concepts. Each activity is designed to keep you aligned with your greater self.

The life each of us lives is the life within the limits of our own thinking. To have life more abundant, we must think in limitless terms of abundance.

~Thomas Dreier

V
Transformation Shifts: Tools for Transformation & Co-Creation with the Universe

The morning of life is like the dawn of a day, full of purity, visions, and harmony.
~Chateubriand

CHAPTER 6

Lifting Your Vibration: Developing Enlightened Thinking Habits

I keep the telephone of my mind open to peace, harmony, health, love, and abundance. Then, whenever doubt, anxiety, or fear try to call me, they will keep getting a busy signal—and soon they'll forget my number.

~Edith Armstrong

Enlightened Thinking Habits

This chapter gives you fifteen cognitive tools (cTools) for imprinting and reinforcing your targeted beliefs and thoughts. Use these to keep your thinking habits aligned with your emergent self.

Remember that your mental muscles can be as resistant to change as your physical muscles. Here's an example. Try to move your little finger without moving your other fingers. Unless you've been practicing doing this, you probably won't be able to. Now fold your arms in front of you; then switch arms. This probably feels awkward and unnatural. Our mental muscles act in the same way. It takes practice. Commitment and practice!

The exercises below will help you make the new thought processes your own. After a while, the new thinking habits will feel as natural to you as the air you breathe.

Conscious Intention

First and most important is having the conscious intention to create change in your life. You need *genuinely* to want the changes, to be serious about making the changes. It is mandatory that you have a firm resolve and reach a definite decision point.

For instance, if you're starting with the Health/Fitness dimension and are trying to lose weight, you need to reach a point in your mind where you mean business. A flimsy, half-hearted commitment will get you nowhere, no matter how many tools for success you master.

Commit to change now! Make up your mind, or put this book down and go mesmerize yourself in front of the television screen. Conscious change absolutely will not happen until you're ready.

Once you make a decision, the universe conspires to make it happen.
~Ralph Waldo Emerson

If you're still with me, then let's move on.

Core Beliefs of Empowerment

Intellectually, you're committed to the five-star belief cluster you were introduced to in the previous chapter. Each morning for the next thirty days, start your day by spending three minutes reflecting on these messages:

- I believe in the power to improve my life.
- I believe in the Universe and my emergent self.
- I believe in myself, my capabilities, and my service or product.
- I believe my efforts are making a difference even when I see no tangible results.
- I believe I deserve success and happiness.

Enter these messages now on your iPhone, Android, or iPad. You can voice-record them, put them in your calendar, or both. Besides reflecting each morning on their powerful content, you should let them penetrate your consciousness each night before you drop off to sleep. By pondering these messages early morning, you set the tone for the whole day. Letting them seep into your mind throughout the night will strengthen your resolve and commitment.

Next, follow through on the five steps below.

Step 1

If you haven't already, memorize your target cluster affirmations (i.e., Wealth/Fiscal Fitness, Relationships, Health/Fitness, etc.). ***Do this now!*** If you like, you can rephrase the statements to fit your particular situation; however, be sure and retain the original messages. I can't emphasize this enough. The new thought patterns need to start becoming a part of your mental makeup. You can only think with the stock of thoughts you have on hand.

Step 2

Read through the fifteen cTools below.

cTools

cTool 1: Shift your focus.

Stay focused on the target beliefs. Whatever you focus on expands, pushing out the things you don't want. For example, if you targeted fitness for improvement, you would keep your attention and focus on its messages, e.g., "I treat my body with the respect it deserves" . . . "I enjoy staying healthy" . . . and so on. Blot out the old messages by consciously focusing on your new belief cluster.

cTool 2: Use opposites.

When limiting beliefs and doubts creep into your consciousness, void them by plugging in their opposites. For example, replace "I'll never lose weight and keep off this blubber" with "I am slim and fit. I can definitely do this!"

cTool 3: Make a part of your regular routine.

Run the new empowering beliefs through your mind at regular intervals throughout the day, e.g., while showering, cleaning, cooking, commuting. By doing this, you'll be reinforcing the new wave patterns in your brain.

cTool 4: Use a thought stoppage mantra.

When negative thoughts and worries come up, have a mantra ready to expel them. One I like is "I trust myself." Or, "I'm better than this." Let go and relax into the moment. The key is to decide on a mantra ahead of time to repeat and use.

cTool 5: Take charge of your Calling Power.

How are you calling life? Are you letting others define who you are?

Take back your power. Stop agreeing with others' negative judgments. Check the labels you're using to define yourself and events. Avoid labeling as a failure anything that happens to you. Reframe it as feedback, a learning experience, or a mistake.

In reality, everything that happens to us is an opportunity—a challenge to make us better.

Your perceptions and interpretations of events become your beliefs. If every time something goes wrong, you view it as a personal failure, then you corrode your self-esteem and self-worth. Take charge of how you define life's situations.

If you want to see dramatic changes in your life, take charge of your calling power. Remember, it's your life and your call!

cTool 6: Use Power Questions to weed out toxic beliefs.

When a limiting belief or thought surfaces in your mind, ask yourself if this belief is serving you.

- Is it making my life happier?

- Is it helping me achieve my important goals?
- Is it triggering positive emotions?
- Is it helping me move in the direction of my big dream?

If the answers to these questions are No, then consciously dismiss beliefs and thoughts that aren't serving you and call up the new ones you previously targeted for improvement.

cTool 7: Throw a wrench into those polluted thought streams.

When angry thoughts start skidding out of control, visualize a monkey wrench taking them out. See them splatter and fall by the wayside.

cTool 8: Make regular use of Belief Boosters.

One mighty belief booster is what I've called Mental Convincers. Your beliefs do not stand alone in your mind but have a whole cluster of supportive thoughts attached to them. Convincers back up the new, more-empowering beliefs by asking "Why," and act as rebuttals against the old self-defeating beliefs.

For example, ask yourself, "Why do I deserve success?" You might hear your inner voice saying, "I've worked hard for this. I've earned a better life. I've experienced all kinds of hardships and setbacks without falling apart. I deserve life's gifts." *Thought clusters such as these will prop up and solidify the new, empowering beliefs.*

This tool is perfect for a variety of issues such as procrastination, getting unstuck, rejection, failure, and relationship issues.

cTool 9: Develop perspective beliefs, or what I call "Shift & Change."

When one area of your life goes awry (e.g., your financial situation), remind yourself that this is just one dimension within a much larger picture. Don't forget your family, your personal relationships, your training and special skills, your creativity, the mighty spiritual realm, plus all the positive qualities you possess, such as honesty, kindness, and initiative.

Shift your focus to those areas of your life that are going well. You can best take care of any current problem by keeping your perspective and refusing to let it bring you down. Whatever we focus on expands. You know this, but how soon we forget! If you constantly focus on what's wrong in your life rather than what's right, you'll only magnify and increase your difficulties.

Recognize that your finances, your relationships, your career, and all the other vital dimensions of your life will always be in various states of flux—sometimes good, sometimes not so good. Rarely will everything be going exactly as you'd like. Reproaching yourself every time one aspect of your life is less than perfect only punctures your self-esteem and makes matters worse. You have the power to influence the fluctuations of your life—to shape and mold them into your desires and dreams.

Your perceptions of and viewpoint on what happens make all the difference. The great philosopher Epictetus once said, "Men are disturbed not by things but by the view which they take of them." Those destined for success rarely let circumstances bother them too much or get the best of them.

cTool 10: Fast-forward your life.

Recognize that the unwanted situation is *temporary;* it's not going to last forever. Life means change. Fast-forward time beyond the event. Picture yourself with the results you want.

Always, always, pat yourself on the back for having the courage to make the effort—regardless of how things turn out.

cTool 11: Be an impartial observer.

Listen to yourself. Step free of your inner chatter and simply watch your thoughts. Don't fight them, don't argue with them, and, by all means, don't try rationalizing them away. Simply let your mind say what it will, but become the observer, not the participant.

This act will put you back in your miracle space, free you from any damaging emotional discharges, and position you for making the right choices from this moment forward.

cTool 12: Command yourself!

Sometimes we just need to order ourselves to shape up. If you tend to be a left-brained individual, you'll find this technique works especially well. Here are a few sample messages to give yourself when you're going off the path of your purpose. These messages should always be short, pithy, and forceful.

- Stop! Enough already!
- It's time! I've had it with this nonsense!
- That's it! It's over. Now is the time to move on to a better life.
- I can do this . . . starting this minute!
- No more excuses! I'm creating my life exactly as I want it.

cTool 13: Zoom out.

Sometimes we get so caught up in our daily problems, we become blind to the larger picture. Our conscious awareness shrinks, and we become trapped in an emotional cloud of hopelessness.

When this occurs, zoom out to capture the greater picture of life. Take out your vision statement. See the possibilities and budding potential of your life.

cTool 14: Do mental aerobics.

Your mind needs nourishment in order to grow, adapt to change, and keep you continually positioned to weed out beliefs and thoughts not in sync with your true self. Good mental activities will also keep you more alert, as well as help ward off memory loss associated with aging.

When your mind becomes sluggish, then your energy level wanes, and you just won't feel up to directing your life's course and making things happen. You're more vulnerable to others' directives that may be totally out of step with your mission.

Work crossword puzzles, Sudoku, and other mind games that are readily available. If you haven't already, download mind power apps on your iPhone, iPad, or iPod for quick access.

cTool 15: Play back a happy moment.

When unwelcome thoughts attempt to gain entrance, step into the mood of your happiest moment in life, e.g., winning an award, getting a promotion or a new job, graduation day, being nominated for an office, the birth of a child. This is an easy-to-use strategy very effective in shifting you from a gloomy humor to a more joyous sentiment.

Step 3

Select and highlight those cTools that resonate most with you. Remember, you are always at the helm in determining what works best for you. Experiment with them, learn from them, adapt them to your particular situation. At the same time, keep an open mind to new potentials and the spirit of transformation.

Step 4

Do some time blocking. Follow through on the strategies you've highlighted above over the next twenty-four hours. Mark specific times in your calendar for each, and set your timer.

Step 5

Gift yourself by doing something special for yourself after the completion of Step 4. This needn't be anything big; however, make it a gift you genuinely want, as simple as taking an hour just for yourself, getting a massage, or having dinner with a friend.

Actually, as your evolution unfolds through committing to these changes, your new perspective and rhythm will be its own reward. Nonetheless, gifting yourself as you progress through the activities helps sustain your momentum. And you deserve it!

Commitment and consistency in using the above strategies is the key! Persevere!

If we are facing in the right direction, all we have to do is keep on walking.
~Buddhist saying

CHAPTER 7

Feeling the Wave: Emotive Strategies

You cannot know what you do not feel.
~Myra Mannes

Emotive Strategies

These strategies are all about your affective realm and feeling state. You want to come to a place in yourself where you deeply and strongly feel the current of the new vibration, the new thought clusters and beliefs. Your aim is to reach a point where you totally own the new thinking patterns. They are no longer just an abstract intellectual understanding, but part of every ounce of your being, a status where you have become one with the great wave of life.

While you'll be using the emotive tools (eTools) in this chapter for only one area right now, keep in mind that these strategies can be used for any of the dimensions of your life that you later target for improvement. These are all very simple and easy to master. It's just this simplicity that makes them so effective.

The big question is: just how do you go about "feeling" an emotion that may be the opposite of your habitual emotional responses? I've provided a variety of scenarios to generate feeling states conducive to bringing in the new thought cluster. Experiment with each of them, then select two or three that are the best fit for you personally. Remember that your thoughts generate feelings and the reverse is also true—your feelings generate thoughts, in an ongoing, back-and-forth process.

As in the previous chapter, follow these five basic steps:

Step 1

You have committed your target belief cluster to memory; now it's time to emote it. Keep a copy of its messages in front of you as you do the exercises.

Step 2

Review and try out the thirteen emotive tools (eTools) below. You'll find that some will come easily, while others may prove more challenging. Use your imagination to call up the images and feelings as best you can.

Keep in mind also that it isn't necessary to understand how they work for them to be effective.

eTools

eTool 1: Imagine it's morning.

You're nude in a very cold climate; your body is shivering from snow and sleet. Then you catch a glimpse of a glow atop a mountain. As the glow rises, express your belief cluster out loud while feeling the soothing warmth of the golden sun ascending into the clear blue sky. Allow yourself to stop shivering and bask in its rays. You feel warm, safe, and secure. All is well with the world.

Keep repeating your thought cluster as you savor the warm glow of the sun. Let the impact of the words' meaning penetrate your skin.

eTool 2: Pretend you're hurting.

You are feeling a raw emptiness deep inside that doesn't want to go away. Allow yourself to feel the hurt; then close your eyes and let yourself feel a wave of gratitude for the power of your emotions. Consciously dissolve the hurt as gratitude sweeps through your body.

Repeat the thought cluster as the feeling of gratitude engulfs you.

eTool 3: Recall a milestone.

Recapture a milestone in your life, a time when you felt on top of the world.

Repeat the thought cluster while feeling jubilant.

eTool 4: Reach deep inside yourself.

Feel the amazing movement of your brain's neuronal messages traveling throughout your body. Mentally let yourself go and feel the tingle and excitement and wonder of your remarkable body.

Repeat the thought cluster as you marvel in the miracle of your internal processes.

eTool 5: Let yourself fly.

Catch the feeling of a bird soaring through the air. See it flying from tree to tree. Feel yourself, light and winged, gliding across the treetops.

Stay with this feeling as you repeat the thought cluster.

eTool 6: Stand in a meadow.

The deep green grass has been freshly mowed, and, as you inhale its delicious scent, you feel free and expansive.

Repeat the thought cluster while taking in the fresh fragrance of the meadow.

eTool 7: Picture a parasailor.

As she soars over the ocean, the waves swell and shrink below. Let yourself feel her awe and freedom.

Repeat the thought cluster to yourself while feeling the grandeur of this moment.

eTool 8: Notice a baby.

A mother passes by with a tiny newborn in her arms. You feel the warm glow of the miracle of birth.

Repeat the thought cluster as you stay within this miracle moment.

eTool 9: Observe the ripples.

As you watch, a young boy throws a pebble into a lake. Let yourself follow the circle of ripples until they disappear.

Quietly repeat the thought cluster as you feel the magic of nature. Feel the moment expand with the circle of ripples.

eTool 10: Touch a flower.

Close your eyes and visualize feeling the soft smooth petals of a plumeria blossom. Inhale its sweet fragrance.

Ponder the thought cluster as you continue to inhale.

eTool 11: Create a tingle.

Make a sliding steeple with your fingertips, gliding them up and down along your palm. Feel the sensation.

Repeat the thought cluster as you alternate between your palms.

eTool 12: Light a candle.

Follow the flame's movement as you affirm the thought cluster.

Feel the rhythm of the flame while continuing to repeat the thought cluster.

eTool 13: Experience the affection of a pet.

You have just returned home from a grueling day at work. Your puppy greets you enthusiastically, wagging his tail and showering you with love. In that magic moment, the worries of the day melt away.

Repeat the thought cluster as you recreate this scene in your mind's eye.

Step 3

Select and highlight the eTools that resonate most with you. Always remember that you are your own best guide. Any instruction or aid is there solely to facilitate your evolution. Filter out any tools that feel off-center for you. At the same time, give yourself the opportunity to try out new approaches.

Step 4

Do some time blocking. Over the next two days, set aside a time to apply the strategies you have highlighted. Enter these times in your calendar.

Step 5

Gift yourself by doing something special for yourself after completing the activities, as described in the previous chapter. You deserve it!

Commitment and consistency in using the above strategies is the key! Persevere!

With ordinary talent and extraordinary perseverance, all things are attainable.

~Thomas Foxwell Buxton

CHAPTER 8

Syncing with Rhythms: Sound Tools

Music . . . is like a great dynamic sun in the center of a solar system which sends out its rays and inspiration in every direction. . . . Music makes us feel that the heavens open and a divine voice calls. Something in our souls responds and understands.

~Leopold Stokowski

Rhythms of Life

A variety of sounds can be used to boost your wave's supremacy in your life, and keep you on the path of greatness. Nature's enchanting sounds and gentle music are exceptionally powerful. Install apps with the soothing sounds of nature. Some you'll want to include are forest sounds, ocean waves, and waterfalls. Put these on your iPhone, Android, iPod, or iPad to have handy. You will also find apps for some of the other sounds I've suggested below. Many of these can be uploaded to your device for free or a nominal fee.

As in the previous chapter, follow these steps:

Step 1

If you have been consistently persevering with the assignments, your target belief cluster is by now comfortably contained within your consciousness. We move forward. With the following rhythm activities as a backdrop, let go and enter the pulse of your truest and greatest self.

Step 2

Read through the seven acoustical tools (aTools) below.

aTools

aTool 1: Listen to an uplifting tune.

This should have no lyrics. Feel the rhythm's vibration percolate throughout your body.

Repeat the thought cluster you have targeted as the rhythm penetrates your body.

aTool 2: Go to a peaceful forest.

Find a place where you can hear the calming sounds of the forest. If such a venue is not near, use one of the forest nature apps you've installed on your device.

Relax, take three deep breaths, and mentally repeat your thought cluster as the enchanting sounds of the forest fill your inner space.

aTool 3: Wash away your worries with ocean waves.

If you do not live near the ocean, try this: close your eyes and cup the palm of your hands over your ears. Listen to the soothing sound of ocean waves playing inside your head. Can you hear them? Or use one of the ocean sound apps you've installed.

As the calming sounds play, slowly repeat your target affirmations.

aTool 4: Listen to a happy baby's soft cooing.

Delight in this joyful sound as you empower yourself with your target cluster of beliefs. And, yes, there's even an app for this.

Repeat the messages as you listen to the gentle sounds.

aTool 5: Stand beside a waterfall.

Listen carefully and feel the magic of the captivating sounds of the droplets splashing beneath.

Silently and steadily repeat the target messages as you bask in the cascade of rhythms.

aTool 6: Hear the wind breathing kindly through the treetops.

Pause within the moment, inhaling the gentle breezes.

Affirm your new belief cluster as you perceive this soft sound.

aTool 7. Go to a grade school playground or park.

Find a place where you can watch young children happily playing and laughing.

As you revel in their carefree happiness, ponder the messages you have targeted.

Other sound tools you may want to consider are Tibetan chants, Beethoven symphonies, gentle drumbeats, and inspiring harp rhythms.

Sound, as vibration, is the very basis of creation and evolution, and will not only help you stay in sync with your higher self, but also boost your mood and keep you healthy.

Rhythm and harmony find their way into the inward places of the soul.

~Plato

Step 3

Select and highlight the rhythm tools above that resonate with you.

Step 4

Do some time blocking. Over the next three days, set aside several times to apply the sound strategies you have highlighted. Mark these times in your calendar now. Continue to practice regularly.

Step 5

Gift yourself by doing something special for yourself after completing the activities. You deserve it!

Commitment and consistency in using the above strategies is the key! Persevere!

Patience and perseverance have a magical effect before which difficulties disappear and obstacles vanish.
~John Quincy Adams

CHAPTER 9

Physical Shift Tools: Body Tools for Shifting to Your New Self

Movement is a medicine for creating change in one's physical, emotional, and mental states.
~Carol Welch

These activities will assist you in stopping the flow of any remaining rampant thoughts invading your consciousness, while shifting to your new self. They are particularly effective when you're feeling anxious, worried, or uneasy about something in your life.

I encourage you also to generate your own physical shift tools with exercises or activities you might already be doing. Use the ones below as a springboard to your own inspirations.

The idea is to get out of your head full of unproductive thought clusters and into your new thought vibrations. You want the new thought sensations to become automatic and routine to you, who you are.

Loosen Up

You've probably the term "loosen up" in one form or another. And it's not especially flattering to hear with the implication that you're uptight.

Let's examine the concept more closely. "Loosen," as I'm using it, means letting go—releasing the tight framework of your mind with its enclosed limiting beliefs and thoughts, all running merrily along in their usual conditioned patterns, totally out of step with the real you. You've observed this happening and maybe tried to stop it, without success.

Loosen up is not about *trying* to change your mind or thoughts. Trying to superimpose your will can only meet with resistance and frustration.

Use your physical body instead. When your mind is tight, most often so is your body. Likewise, when you relax and loosen up your body, your mind responds in kind.

Do the physical activities below. Focusing on your body movements halts your thought stream. As your mind is cleared of toxic self-talk, repeat your targeted cluster of affirmations. A couple of these exercises may sound silly to you. That's irrelevant. What matters is their results.

As in the previous chapters, follow these steps:

Step 1

Continue with the area of your life you have targeted for improvement. By this time, you should be effortlessly calling up your belief cluster several times throughout each day.

Step 2

Read through the ten physical tools (pTools) below.

pTools

pTool 1: Body Roll

Stand tall, arms held limply by your sides. Now go through a body roll from top to bottom, shaking each part of your body—your arms, hands, upper torso, buttocks, legs, and feet—then your whole body.

Repeat your targeted thought cluster twice as you perform the Body Roll.

pTool 2: Aerobic Dance

If you enjoy dance, put on a YouTube dance video you find appealing and do one of the upbeat routines—zumba, salsa, or a fast-paced ballroom dance.

While dancing, run the thought cluster through your mind.

pTool3: Water Magic

Immerse yourself completely in water. There's something very potent about being surrounded by water. If you have a swimming pool, a lake, or an ocean nearby, wonderful! If not, use your bathtub or shower. Immerse yourself in the water and flap freely.

If you absolutely cannot or don't want to take time for full body immersion, then simply get up and go to your washbasin and splash cold water on your face. I'm talking about a lot, not a few drops. Cup your hands and fully splash your face several times.

Repeat your affirmation cluster as you immerse yourself.

pTool 4: Jump

Jump up and down several times. Feel the bounce and movement of your body.

Run the thought cluster through your mind while jumping.

pTool 5: Walk

Take a brisk ten-minute walk, preferably by a stream or waterfall, or through a meadow, woods, flower garden, or park. Get outside your head and notice nature's delights.

Repeat the thought cluster while walking.

pTool 6: Skip Rope

Skip rope for three to five minutes. This is an excellent exercise that can be done almost anywhere: at home, at a playground, or in a hotel room if you're traveling.

Shift your focus to the rope skipping and repeat your thought cluster.

pTool 7: Yoga

If you've never tried yoga, I highly recommend it. Most

communities offer yoga classes for a nominal fee. Try a free trial session to see if it's right for you.

During a yoga session, mentally repeat your targeted belief cluster.

pTool 8: Balance

Balance yourself on one foot and hold that pose for five to ten seconds. This is a simple act that is quick, easy, and effective for shifting your focus away from your worries and onto the act of balancing.

Once you feel steady, repeat your thought cluster.

pTool 9: Team Sports

Team sports such as tennis, basketball, baseball, and soccer can be effective also. Their drawback is the need to schedule with others in advance. If you're trying to shake off a bad mood or big disappointment, you need something in place you can do right now, not tomorrow or next week. In this case, refer to a pTool you can immediately apply.

pTool 10: Other Activities

Cycling, rowing, tennis, and hiking are all possibilities to consider if available to you.

Repeat the thought cluster at regular intervals while doing one of these activities.

Step 3

Select and highlight the pTools that match your interests and inclinations. There is no set "right" activity to do in this step. What makes the difference is the physical movement itself, and the way it can help take the focus off any rampant thoughts threatening your welfare.

Note: Depending on your physical condition and age, only perform those activities that feel comfortable to you. If in doubt, consult with your physician. Before beginning any physical movement routine, get a green light from your doctor.

Step 4

Do some time blocking. Over the next week, set aside a time to apply the above strategies you have highlighted. Mark specific times in your calendar now.

Step 5

Gift yourself by doing something special for yourself after completing the activities. You deserve it!

Commitment and consistency in using the above strategies is the key! Persevere!

The flower that follows the sun does so even on cloudy days.
~Robert Leighton

VI
Mastering Triggers

If one practices . . . one will attain to that power which is latent in every soul.
~Hazrat Inayat Khan

CHAPTER 10

Triumphing Over Triggers

How people treat you is their karma; how you react is yours.
~Wayne Dyer

Preparation for Life's Triggers

In this chapter, I'll be giving you some simple steps for managing any damaging triggers disrupting your happiness and well-being.

Triggers are those stimuli that, through past conditioning, set off a string of thoughts in your mind, triggering a reaction, first in thought, then in emotion, and then frequently in the actions you do or don't take.

Some common triggers that try us are rejections, a flight delay, food commercials, cigarette smoke, a critical remark, or a disappointing event. A trigger can also be what someone doesn't say or do.

Certain triggers may produce relatively weak reactions in you; others, stronger reactions. However, a host of unchecked mild trigger-reactions can add up to big troubles. Without effective remedial tools on hand, even the mild daily annoyances and irritations you experience from triggers can undermine your happiness and keep you from living life to its fullest.

Below are just a few examples of trigger-reaction links from the major dimensions we looked at earlier: Career/Financial, Relationships, and Physical Fitness.

After reviewing them, you'll be asked to come up with those that are impeding your success and peace of mind. Next, you'll learn some quick action steps to thwart them and stay in sync with your wave rhythm.

Common Career/Financial Triggers:

- Your boss unfairly criticizes you.
- You didn't get the raise you were expecting.
- Your credit cards are maxed out, and you're barely scraping by.
- You're behind on your house payment, and the mortgage company is breathing down your neck.
- Your car is falling apart and you can't afford a new one.
- You get rejected for a job. Another one!

If any of the above are true for you, how are you handling them in your head? Most people without any mind training let themselves be taken over by limiting thoughts that breed discouragement and unproductive action.

What thoughts and feelings do you find flashing through your mind? "I'm a failure" . . . "I'll never get out of debt" . . . "life is hard" . . . "the economy is bad" . . . "there's nothing I can do" . . . "life's a struggle" . . . ?

Yes, these situations can be all too true and real in your life. The economy may be bad, your employer may unjustly criticize you, and your financial situation may be dire. Remember, however, that your own interpretations and thoughts—not the situation—lead to your emotions and actions. If you're continually telling yourself that you're a failure or can't do anything right or will never get out of debt, these become self-fulfilling prophecies.

The objective in this chapter is to break free from any obstinate limiting thoughts triggered by your particular situation, and to plug in new thought sequences that align with your real self. Once you become skilled at making this shift, you'll find that unwanted events in your life will begin falling by the wayside.

Common Relationship Triggers:

- You spend hours getting dressed to go out, put on a new dress, and are looking good. Your significant other is mute, when, of course, he should be telling you how terrific you look.

- You return from the beauty salon and have a fantastic new hairstyle. Your sweetheart doesn't notice.
- Your spouse forgets your birthday or anniversary.
- Out on a new date with a hunk, you start thinking, "He'll never be interested in me. I'll probably say something stupid. These first dates never work out . . . ."
- You go out with a great guy and have a super time. You're looking forward to seeing him again, but, two weeks later, he still hasn't called.
- You get rejected by a loved one.
- Your mate belittles you in front of others.
- Your sweetheart never shows any appreciation for all the things you do.
- Your partner gives you nil support on your important goals.

Do any of the above sound familiar? How are you responding? With irritation, annoyance, anger?

Yes, he certainly should shape up and not be so insensitive, thoughtless, and uncaring. But you know perfectly well that's not likely to happen within the current dynamics of your relationship. And you also know that others are responsible for their own behavior; thus, trying to "change them" is rarely the smart approach.

So, the task at hand is not to change your spouse, sweetheart, or the inconsiderate men that come into your life. Rather, your arena of concern is your own thoughts and reactions. This is what you have control over, and this is where your focus needs to be. This is where your peace of mind and happiness lie.

When we are no longer able to change a situation, we are challenged to change ourselves.

~Victor Frankl

Common Food and Fitness Triggers:

- While watching television, a dessert commercial triggers the thought and image of that delicious cherry pie in your frig. "Yum, the piece I had for dinner was soo good, and it was just a little slice. . . ." Without hesitation, you find yourself heading for the kitchen.
- The treadmill collecting cobwebs in your den mocks you. "Hey, shut up," you say. "I tried you, and didn't lose an ounce! Besides you're boring. Too much work. Later."
- Maybe you attempted to quit smoking or to stop drinking too much, and, after a few failures, the voice inside your head scoffs, "This is just the way I am. It's futile to try." Or, even more commonly, "Now's not a good time."
- Hubby sits munching cashew peanuts while you're trying to read. He knows you love cashews and are attempting to diet. "What is his problem?! Sheesh, they smell good! How am I ever going to lose weight with his inconsiderateness?"

With this recurring battery of thoughts, you're no match for an appetizing dessert, snack, or cigarette trigger. Your past conditioning predisposes you to respond in the same old ways. Maybe you can succeed in white-knuckling it for awhile, but, when the stressors pile up—kaput, it's over!

We wouldn't dream of going into a battlefield without the proper equipment to protect ourselves; yet, when it comes to our own internal "minefields," most of us arrive empty-minded. We're not stocked with the mental gear that could save us from the battle of the bulge, financial despair, or any of the many unfortunate triggers that parade through our days. Nor are we ready with the perceptive equipment that could save us from anger, resentment, bitterness, discouragement, and disillusion. We find ourselves totally unprepared for the barrage of potent triggers that come our way.

To break free from these unwanted links, you must come equipped with a new reserve of interpretations and thoughts.

Throughout this book you have been learning how to stock yourself with the mind processes and strategies that can defeat the buildup of unhealthy mental plaque. If you've been applying them consistently, you are already feeling the triumphant magic of your new life rhythm.

Still, some of the stressors you're facing may continue to test and dampen your spirits. Take the quick action steps below to disband those troublesome trigger-reaction links persisting in your life.

In the process, you'll be revitalizing and reinforcing your new wave patterns. Once the new patterns are permanently established, you'll find them just as tough to break as the old ways have been.

The remarkable thing about staying in tune with your authentic wave pattern is that it's resilient in the face of change and adept at transforming all the undesired events thrown into your path. Rather than arguing, rationalizing, justifying, and getting upset, you glide smoothly through them. You live seamlessly on a different plane of being, your best self at the helm. With this presence of mind and emotion, you are poised to make those choices that both enrich your life and the lives of others.

Please take the time to complete the steps below. You're almost there!

Quick Action Steps

Step 1

A. Identify triggers in your life that are setting off a train of limiting thoughts.

Begin by recognizing five key external triggers. As in the above examples, this might be a job or relationship disappointment, a difficult person's comments, someone's critical remarks, poor service at a restaurant or store, or crazy drivers on the road. Be specific. Your thought- and thinking-triggers are tied to specific events. Be careful not to fall into justifying your position and actions based on the situation. As logical as that may seem at the time, it is not serving your interests.

Allowing someone's rude comments or bad behavior to anger or upset you makes no sense. It only appears natural because it's been your customary response. You've learned that it's okay to react. Remember: "They have the problem, not me." It's just plain foolish to make it your problem.

Next, target any internal triggers that have recently set off an unhealthy thought chain. Frequently these come from not living up to your own inner standards, or all the "shoulds" and "should nots" you've been feeding yourself. For example, you'd vowed to take off ten pounds and then just devoured a bag of chocolates. You chastise yourself with a barrage of nonproductive thoughts: "Darn, there I go again. How am I ever going to get rid of all this blubber?" Emotional feelings of discouragement, guilt, and disillusionment ensue.

Write down the personal triggers that spring to mind from the life dimension you've targeted.

B. The second part of Step 1 is **unconditional acceptance** of wherever you are now. You've heard this over and over, yet so many of us still struggle with it. Be compassionate with yourself! You are an amazing, miraculous being, no matter what—no matter what your weight, your so-called failures, your financial situation, or what bad things you think you've done in the past.

This is a new day, and a new you is emerging with each sunrise. Complete the self-acceptance process by daily patting yourself on the back for all the things you're doing right, no matter how small. I know there are many. Look for them and feel good about yourself!

The most terrifying thing is to accept oneself completely.
~C. G. Jung

Step 2

Remind yourself again and again that it's your *perceptions and interpretations* of the situation that are the critical link to your reactions. It has nothing to do with how someone treats you, how poor service is, or how bad the economy is. And it has nothing to do with what you do (smoke too much, eat too much, drink too much, watch too much television). It's how you're *internally defining* the event that knocks you off your wave and back into the mine pits of despair.

When you do something that's contrary to your mental ideal of what you think you should be doing, your recurring thought streams will determine what results you'll have in the future, i.e., whether you'll continue down the same wasteful beaten path, or break free from the triggers with new constructive responses—and allow the authentic rhythm of yourself to take over.

Step 3

Decide which of the tools you've mastered to call up when a trigger occurs. As we've noted throughout this book, this is a decision that must be made prior to exposure to any of your potential triggers. Your triggers set off thoughts in a flash! You must have your mind stocked with the appropriate remedial tools. They must be on the tip of your mental tongue, ready to launch!

In selecting your strategies, especially go back to the material on "Lifting your Vibration" (Chapter 6) and "Feeling the Wave" (Chapter 7). Review the tools you've highlighted and practiced in these chapters, adding any new ones applicable to your particular triggers. Yes, this takes a little time, but the payoff is decidedly worth it. You want your life to change, right?

Here are a couple of examples to get you started:

Trigger Scenario 1: You've just experienced a big disappointment (didn't get the job, the raise, the guy, etc.).

Enter cTool 9: "Shift & Change"—shift your focus to the areas of your life that are going well. Remind yourself that what you focus on, expands. Keep your perspective: this event is temporary **(cTool 10).** Think past it to your desired vision. Pat yourself on the back for making the effort!

To counteract your feelings of discouragement, use **eTool 3**: "Recall a milestone." Recreate this in your mind now. Bask in the joy of that moment.

Next, boost your mood with one of the **sound tools**, e.g., **aTool 1:**

"Listen to an uplifting tune," or **aTool 2**: "Go to a peaceful forest." Sound tools are exceptionally powerful in shaking you free from a frustrating setback.

Trigger Scenario 2: You just got back from vacation, step on your bathroom scale, and can't believe your eyes!

"Ouch, how could I have gained that much in two weeks?!" A flood of self-reprimands start taking over your peace of mind. "Here I starved myself to lose weight before going on vacation, and now it's all back, and more! How the heck did that happen! I didn't eat that much." You move your bathroom scale to another spot on the floor and very gingerly step on again. You take off your panties and jewelry. Nada, no change; the pounds are still there glaring at you. "It's humiliating and friggin' frustrating!"

Enter cTool 4: Use a thought stoppage mantra. Blast out the barrage of thoughts with a mantra: "I had a terrific trip. I trust myself to change. I will persist until I succeed. I am becoming slim from this moment forward."

Notice the acceptance: "This is where I am right now, and that's okay. The past doesn't equal the future."

Enter cTool 11: "Be an impartial observer." Listen to yourself. Step free of your inner chatter and simply watch your thoughts. Don't fight them, don't argue with them, and, by all means, don't try rationalizing them away. Simply let your mind say what it will, but become the observer, not the participant. This act will put you back in your miracle space, free you from any damaging emotional discharges, and position you for making the right choices from this moment forward.

Enter pTool 5: "Walk." Take a ten minute walk. Bravo! You've taken a solid step toward change. Applaud yourself!

Notice that you often will want to make use of more than one tool for maximum effectiveness. Other tools highly effective for **Trigger Scenario 2** are the **Focus Shifts** you learned in Chapter 4.

Don't let the simplicity of these strategies delude you into doubting their effectiveness. Tiny mind shifts can create enormous results in your life!

Step 4

After identifying the problematic triggers, **mentally rehearse** the resolution of each through use of the strategies you've selected. Studies have shown that mental rehearsal can be just as effective as the act itself.

The process is very simple: make a list of the triggers that are sparking the old patterns, then decide on the best tools to offset them.

Think through the situations that have occurred in the past and provoked you. If these same or similar situations are likely to occur in the future, decide how you're going to respond. That is, decide now which of the strategies you've practiced will work best for you in each situation. Then just do it. That's really all there is to it.

Reaching a definite decision point on each trigger is the first key. The same trigger-reactions tend to occur over and over again; we're likely to respond in the same limiting ways to similar scenes in our life. To initiate a new, more constructive response, you need to break the cycle.

The second key is practice. Without the mental rehearsal and practice to create a new pattern, the past brain circuits will continue to override your good intentions. They're stronger because they've been used so frequently. You have to build up the mental-emotional muscle for the new circuits before they can dominate and become your automatic reactions to events—before they become authentically you.

Step 5

Finally, **block out time**, either completing each of the above steps now, or marking your calendar with a specific time to follow through. You cannot just read what to do and expect it magically to happen. I repeat: either do it now, or block out a definite time in your calendar to identify, rehearse, and master the new mind links.

Please don't get discouraged. I know some of the changes may be slower than you'd like. Keep your commitment, and continue to do whatever you can. If you only act upon 80% of what I'm recommending, you'll be successful. And if all you can do right now is 25%, you'll be off to a great start! For whatever you do, don't forget to pat yourself on the back and feel good about yourself.

Have patience with all things, but especially with yourself.
~Anonymous

It is high time to close the mine pits of discouragement, anger, resentment, and struggle. You no longer need to dwell under the dark shadows of these fiends. Open your windows and let in the vibrant sunshine of inspiration, joy, and abundance. This is the world for which you were intended.

Change always comes bearing gifts.
~Price Pritchett

If nothing ever changed, there'd be no butterflies.
~Author Unknown

VII
Acting Within Your Authentic Self

Trust only movement. Life happens at the level of events, not of words.
Trust movement.
~Alfred Adler

CHAPTER 11

Acting Within Your New Wave Patterns

Act the part and you will become the part.
~William James

By this time, you are well on your way toward acting within your new wave patterns. This chapter will allow you to complete the process fully.

As you act on the belief clusters, they are reinforced and become permanently stamped in your consciousness. Below are action examples for the three categories we looked at in the last chapter: Financial, Relationships, and Health/Fitness. Your task is then to commit to following through by taking the actions which support the new you.

Note that I have tied each action to specific time blocks. You can modify the time frames to fit your lifestyle; however, you need to decide definitely on an alternative time as you go through each. Write it down and set a date in your calendar to begin the activity. Then set your timer to remind you! Many cell phones have a built-in calendar and timer. If yours doesn't, and you haven't installed such programs already, I strongly recommend that you stop reading and do that now.

Scan the categories below; then begin with the one you targeted earlier. If you have targeted more than one area for improvement, follow through on each after first mastering your initial dimension.

Financial

Ask Yourself:

How does a person who has achieved financial success and happiness act?

Listed below are six fundamental behaviors practiced by those who live successfully, along with specific actions for you to take.

Actions to Take:

- **Expresses appreciation and gratitude daily for all the blessings of life.**

Each morning when you awaken, type or write out five things for which you are grateful. Try to add at least one new item each day. I have been doing this for three years now, and it is the singularly most beneficial action I take to keep me on the path to prosperity.

As an alternative, you can use your voice recorder to express your appreciation. I often use the recorder on my iPhone when traveling.

This simple one-minute action step will set the tone for your whole day and get you off to the right start.

- **Follows through on goals and priorities on a regular basis.**

Block out a minimum of two hours a day, five days a week, at the same time each day, to devote to your creative dream project. Do absolutely nothing else during this time frame. Turn off your phone. Put a "Do Not Disturb" sign on your door. Insofar as possible, shelter yourself from any likely interruptions.

- **Completes projects.**

Nothing is more debilitating then having a lot of unfinished projects laying around. If this is the case for you, choose one high-priority project and block out regular times each week to devote to it. Have a precise date for completion! Put these times in your calendar now.

- **When feeling discouraged or doubtful, accepts the mood and does whatever she can.**

You can always do something, no matter how small, related to your dream project. For example, type an e-mail, make a phone call, update your blog or web site, draft a paragraph for that article or book you've long been intending to write.

Consider the consequences of "not acting." You're only going to feel worse than you do already. Taking even the smallest step in the direction of your dreams and goals will give you an energy boost and lift your mood.

■ **Regularly nourishes her mind with good literature and inspirational and motivational messages.**

Subscribe to an inspirational message in your e-mail each day. Read one good book each month. Check out a web site now to subscribe to a daily inspirational message. Make a list of three books you've been intending to read and obtain a copy of the first one this week.

■ **Takes regular actions in the service of others.**

This can be as simple as making a commitment to perform one "act of kindness" each week, e.g., volunteering online for a community or global organization, assisting a local humanitarian group, or making a donation to a cause you believe in. To help you get started, check out these three web sites.

- Visit http://www.one.org to become part of a worldwide effort to fight disease and global poverty.
- Empower your global neighbors to become economically independent, improve their standard of living, and alleviate poverty for themselves and their communities. Register at http://www.kiva.org.
- Improve your vocabulary and donate rice free through the UN to help end world hunger— http://www.freerice.com.

Decide now what you can do and enter times in your calendar for the next three months. Do whatever you can, even if it's only five minutes a week. The key is deciding what and when.

Remember—whenever you act with kindness in the service of others, it comes back to you threefold.

Relationships

Ask Yourself:

How does someone who desires a better relationship act?

Listed below are specific actions for you to take.

Actions to Take:

■ **If you are in an ongoing relationship that you'd like to improve:**

- Pay your partner a sincere compliment each day for the next two weeks.

This isn't as easy as it sounds if your relationship hasn't been going well. However, with a little reflection, you'll find that you can come up with some compliments that are genuine. We're not looking for lavish praise here, but simple sincere comments like, "You look good in that shirt" or "You did a good job." If you can do this honestly and regularly, you'll be amazed at the results!

Generally speaking, we are treated according to how we treat ourselves and others.

- Create a list of fifteen reasons you are a worthy person and deserve the best. Read it over daily. Next, create a list of at least five reasons your partner is worthy. Read it over daily. If after six weeks your partner is not treating you with the respect you deserve, leave!

If you are moving out of a relationship that's not working and/or are seeking a new relationship:

Research the social or civic organizations in your area, preferably ones that meet several times a month. Join one this week which will allow you to meet potential mates according to your vision statement.

Participate in the group regularly. Prepare yourself beforehand by practicing your Relationships Belief Cluster with one or more of the tools from previous chapters.

Certainly you can meet the person of your dreams by chance, especially if you've been using the strategies I've recommended. Nonetheless, planning and creating opportunities will maximize your success. Be proactive.

Last, ask yourself these questions:

- **Am I focusing too much on having a relationship?**
Sometimes we just need to back off and become involved in activities we enjoy (in which there are potential partners, of course). Shift your focus to having a good time doing the things you love most.
- **Do you feel you need a relationship for your life to be complete?**
You don't. And the flip side is, the more self-fulfilled and happy you are within your own skin, the more likely you'll attract the right person.
- **What kind of life do you want?**
The key to finding a relationship that fulfills your needs is knowing precisely what you want. Go back to your vision statement. Where do you want to live, work, travel? What makes your heart sing?

Health/Physical Fitness

Ask Yourself:

How does someone who maintains a healthy, physically-fit lifestyle act?

Below, I have broken down into separate actions each of the cluster affirmations you've learned. I am not a physician and the recommendations provided are certainly not intended as a full-blown fitness program. The few simple suggested actions will, however, assist you in reinforcing your new thought patterns.

Tip: Most people go overboard when starting a new fitness program, eating too little and exercising too much. Start small. Be consistent and you will see big results. And—remember—always consult with your doctor before starting any new diet or exercise program.

Actions to Take:

■ **I eat those foods that are good for me and the planet.**

Decide on the changes you will make to your diet now. Write these and a start date (no later than two weeks out) in your calendar.

Now, go through your pantry, refrigerator, and freezer, and throw out everything that is unhealthy. You know what they are! If you're sharing food space with others, you'll be doing them a favor as well!

Next, go to Whole Foods Market, Trader Joe's, or a local farmers' market, and purchase foods that your body deserves! You know what they are. While shopping, buy yourself a small dinner platter, no more than three-quarters the size of a regular platter. This will aid you in eating moderately.

Tip: Drink a glass of water before meals. Allow yourself a snack of choice twice a week. The idea is to eat healthy, not deny or starve yourself.

■ **I have a regular physical activity routine that is fun.**

Decide on two or three activities you enjoy doing. What are they? Dancing, swimming, tennis, aerobic classes? Sign up for a weekly class for one, then decide on another activity to do by yourself daily (e.g., walking, biking, jogging, yoga). Do this for twenty minutes each morning before breakfast. Take a ten-minute brisk walk evenings after dinner. Yes, you can!

Tip: Limit watching television to two hours daily. During commercials, stretch, practice yoga, or do sit-ups.

■ **I am at the optimal weight for my height and frame.**

What is your optimal weight? Check a Body Mass Index (BMI) chart if you're not sure. Write it down.

Now write what's realistic to lose per week and month. Calculate what you can realistically lose in three months, and what your new clothing size would be. Then, go out this weekend and buy yourself a gorgeous dress or pair of pants in that size. One that you really, really would like to wear!

Now, I don't want you to put yourself in hock, but this needs to have enough appeal to entice you. If you have budget constraints, check out one of the "nice twice" shops in your area or shop online.

And, yes, I imagine if you're like most women, you have a closet full of clothes that are too tight to wear. They're not a strong enough incentive. You need to go shopping!

Tip: Most people overestimate how much they can lose quickly, and, when they fail, fall into a crippling self-scolding cycle. Start small. Success builds on success.

■ **I enjoy staying healthy.**

The question is: how can you enjoy staying healthy if your past belief system has told you over and over again that exercise is no fun, plus dieting is painful and never works anyway because you just gain it all back? Why bother? You know the all-too-familiar thought track.

Now I know you've been working on your thinking habits, but are there some actions you can take to also help clear out those fatty thought bubbles still hanging around?

Happily, there are! Once your body is clear of all the processed and unhealthy foods in your system, you'll actually crave what's good for you. Honest! Besides, that's all you have in the house, right? You'll love eating fresh fruit and vegetables. Local and organic, I hope. And what about exercise? Remember, I asked you to find a physical activity that's fun. If you haven't done this yet, now's the time!

Begin eating in moderation the healthy foods you have purchased. In no time at all, these will be the foods of choice that you genuinely enjoy eating.

Tip: Keep a fitness magazine on your ebook reader, desk, or coffee table to refer to often. This will help you stay motivated if you get in a slump.

■ **I treat my body with the respect it deserves.**

What does a person who cares about herself and her body do?

All the things I've listed above to keep her body, and mind, well.

She also rewards herself with incremental gifts each week. Yes, you can lose weight without rewarding yourself, but why? You care about yourself enough to give yourself something special for your results. Each week you achieve the desired result, treat yourself. And, no, I don't mean eat a humongous meal that makes you feel all bloated and gassy.

Write down immediately three very special gifts you'd especially like to have. They are to be presented to yourself after each week of success. Then write down one for the next two month's success. Go shopping for them this week!

These needn't be material gifts. How about something special you've been wanting to do, but haven't felt you had the time? These are in addition to the new outfit you have purchased. You do believe in your success, right? My clients are delighted with these recommendations, and have had excellent results.

Tip: For one of your gifts, I recommend a professional massage, a spa treatment, or a mineral bath. Be kind to your body.

Continue to the next chapter only after you have begun taking the successful-living actions to reinforce your new mind shifts.

Commitment leads to action. Action brings your dream closer.
~Marcia Wieder

VIII
Belief Hubs for Ongoing Happiness & Success

Few minds are sunlike, sources of light in themselves and to others: many more are moons that shine with a borrowed radiance. One may easily distinguish the two: the former are always full; the latter only now and then, when their suns are shining full upon them.

~Augustus William Hare and Julius Charles Hare

CHAPTER 12

Empowering Belief Hubs: Staying Aligned with Your Authentic Self

Just as a picture is drawn by an artist, surroundings are created by the activities of the mind.
~The Buddha

Core Beliefs of Empowerment

Each morning you are starting the day with the core beliefs of empowerment you learned earlier. You are also reflecting on their messages as you drift off to sleep at night. They have started to become first nature to you, an inherent part of your internal dialogue.

Below, I expand on the core beliefs at the cornerstone of any endeavor, whether financial and career success, physical/mental health, or maintaining good relationships. I hope that most of these are by now a regular part of your self-talk. If not, go back to the shift strategies you have highlighted and begin making them your own. Understand that this entails more than just agreeing with them. It means living them.

As you mentally and emotionally embrace each message, ask yourself what it means in terms of your life and circumstances. Each hub is vitally important to keep you aligned with your greater self. Take some time to reflect on their meaning and implications for you. When these messages are fully internalized and taken to heart, you will prosper beyond your wildest dreams.

Self-Belief Hub

- I believe in the power to improve my life.
- I believe in the Universe and my emergent self.
- I believe in myself, my capabilities, and my service or product.
- I believe my efforts are making a difference even when I see no tangible results.
- I believe I deserve success and happiness.

Questions to Ask:

What does a full-blown "belief in yourself and your service or product" lead to? Can you feel the power and energy of this belief? Remember, its basis is unconditional self-acceptance.

How does the belief that "your efforts make a difference even when you see no tangible results" play out in your life? Hint: Instead of getting discouraged when the desired change doesn't happen immediately, you remain confident and strong. You continue toward your dreams. You know they are imminent.

What does the realization that "you deserve prosperity and happiness" mean to you? How is it expressed in your day-to-day practices? Are you gifting yourself on a regular basis?

Others-Belief Hub

- I believe it's smart to keep my agreements and act with honesty and integrity.
- I believe I am here to make a contribution to humanity, no matter how small.
- I believe each person, as part of the human family, deserves prosperity and happiness.
- I believe in focusing on my own improvement and choices, and do not waste energy worrying about others' choices and actions.
- I believe in making a positive difference in the lives of others.

Questions to Ask:

In what ways does "keeping your agreements and acting with honesty and integrity" manifest itself in your relationships? Do you only keep your agreements when convenient or expedient? Or do you adhere to a higher standard?

How does the belief that you are "making a positive difference in the lives of others" express itself? By the example you set? Through your work?

Temporal-Belief Hub

- I value my life and time.
- I block out time according to my priorities and goals.
- I take consistent action in the direction of my dreams.
- I spend the bulk of my time on those activities that are enriching and satisfying.
- I celebrate and enjoy the miracle of life.

Questions to Ask:

Where is your time going, and is the bulk of it truly directed toward those activities at the heart of your soul's purpose?

Do you have a flexible time plan for all the important dimensions of your life? Use the guidelines and time blocks provided throughout this book to keep you on the path of prosperity. As your life situation changes, shift your focus accordingly.

Remember to keep your vision statement on your desk or wall, or wherever you spend most of your time. Read it over daily! Take a minimum of one action step each day toward your dream.

How are you celebrating life? Celebration of life doesn't mean simply having fun on holidays and special occasions. Each day, give yourself the gift of joyful living. Remember to keep your focus, and walk within the spotlight of your authentic self.

If you fall short on any of the core beliefs and expressions of empowerment—most of us do—then make a commitment to tweak your lifestyle starting today. Congratulate yourself for the journey you've taken, and the many challenges you've faced.

The rainbows of life follow the storm.
~Anonymous

IX
Riding the Wave

Either you decide to stay in the shallow end of the pool or you go out in the ocean.
~Christopher Reeve

CHAPTER 13

Riding the Great Wave of Life

You must live in the present, launch yourself on every wave,
find your eternity in each moment.
~Henry David Thoreau

All the strategies and steps you've taken thus far have given you the power to stay aligned and in rhythm with your greater self. You are now poised to ride the great wave of life.

The Wave of Life

The wave of life is dynamic, ever expanding, and expresses itself in countless forms and shapes. It is a symphony of beauty and joyful presence, encompassing all time, space, and eternity. The wave of life is antithetical to struggle, hostility, combat, and war.

At the foundation of all the strategies we've been discussing is your unique wave and state of being. As part of the great wave of life, you are empowered with all its vibrational elements. With your free will, you can shape these elements according to your desires and dreams. You can also create new elements. You are a pulse within the larger vibration, or Universal Being. Each of the human waves of life make up a portion of this great wave of life.

Your Spiritual Self versus Your Emotions

You may refer to it as your purest self or spiritual self. Sometimes, however, we get confused about the voices that arise within us, and mix our instinctive needs and emotions with our intuitive feelings. The emotional content of your mind is a separate thing altogether. Emotions spring from our beliefs and thinking processes. Emotions are something we get caught up in, whether it be a negative emotion like anger or the positive emotion of delight.

Psychologists have indeed identified over fifty different emotional states. They are a healthy part of the human experience; we certainly do not want to become stoic and exist without emotions in our lives.

However, as you have learned, we can master our emotional states by taking charge of our beliefs, thinking habits, and thoughts. In this way, we maximize positive, feel-good states, and minimize destructive emotions that would wreak havoc in our lives. We position ourselves for attunement with the wave of life.

People often ask, how do your "emotional states" differ from the spiritual realm? And how do you know the difference?

A spiritual state lies outside any cognitive mind-set and any emotional feeling. Below, I've listed primary qualities of your spiritual state to help you make distinctions between it and your emotions.

In the previous sections, you have learned strategies to aid you in keeping all the elements of your mind—your beliefs, thoughts, and emotions—aligned with your eternal state or your true self, the unique wave of you. When these internal elements are in harmony with your greater self, your actions will also be in accord with the miracle of the Universe. i.e., , your lifestyle will reflect your true self, manifesting the dreams of the heart.

Here, we look at some of the key characteristics of this spiritual state, and summarize some of the basic means that you as a conscious human being can bring into play to dwell fully in this state. Note that I'm using "spiritual state" as synonymous with your true vibrational wave state.

Key Characteristics

A spiritual state
. . . is free of all emotional residue and its by-products.
. . . does not hold beliefs or thoughts.
. . . makes no judgments.
. . . does not try to reason things out by using logic or any cognitive elements.

A spiritual state
. . . is free in the purest sense of the word.
. . . has no boundaries—physical, mental, or emotional.
. . . is expansive.
. . . is all and nothing.

A spiritual state
. . . is timeless.
. . . is where space and matter are inseparable.
. . . is purposeful.
. . . is creative.
. . . is full awareness.

A spiritual state
. . . occupies all living and nonliving creatures, and everything in between.
. . . is beauty and kindness and wonder and playfulness.
. . . is abundance, love, and reverence for life.
. . . travels faster than the speed of light, going nowhere and everywhere.
. . . is always present.

How Do You Recognize It?

You just know. *Really* know.

When in its presence, you have no fear or anxiety or cause for concern.

When in its presence, you know you are safe and protected from harm.
You know that all is well, even when the reflections from your conditioned mind tell you otherwise.
You partake of riches heretofore unknown.

You can feel your energy.
You are attuned to the positive energy of others.
Your awareness is no longer a sliver of the pie, but is the pie expanding.
You are a co-creator with the great wave of life; there is no separation between you and the Universe.
Your choices and actions are in accord with a larger purpose.

How Do You Dwell in Its Presence?

Throughout this book, you've been offered the beliefs, thinking habits, thoughts, and choices that will allow you alignment with the true wave of you, your spiritual self. This is our task on earth: to fine-tune our lives to the rhythm and purpose of the universal self. As we do this, our lives become meaningful, rich, and abundant. We are showered with the blessings of the Universe.

Spiritual Processes to Enter This Realm of Being

Although I'll be separating these out with concepts, they are each part of the same process. Breaking them down into separate components will guide you in realizing them as a whole. I'd like them to serve as prompters and inspirators whenever you find yourself experiencing doubts or fears.

There are only five of these spiritual tools—sTools. They are simple and you've been exposed to them before; none should be new to you. Whole books have been written on each. The list below is meant as a reminder and refresher of what you already know.

Read each through, allowing the meaning to enter fully into your understanding. Then, let go of the concepts completely, along with all thinking and thought. See them as windows to open and explore a new realm of being.

sTools

sTool 1: Intention

This is not a flimsy "I intend to improve my life, lose weight, or become successful . . . someday, somehow, sometime," but a full-blown intention of becoming one with your new self. You are the intention and the action.

When your intent is in accordance with the Universe, things start happening.
~Author Unknown

sTool 2: Surrender

You let go of your will and control. You become one with the Universe. You do not need to try or hope or wish for something. There is nothing else. You only need to be.

If you surrender completely to the moments as they pass, you live more richly those moments.
~Anne Morrow Lindbergh

sTool 3: Trust

As you let go and surrender, you give up all concerns about safety and security. You rest in the arms of the Universe. You are at peace. You are the Universe.

Trust is letting go of needing to know all the details before you open your heart.
~Author Unknown

sTool 4: Open Your Eyes

It has often been said that the eyes are the windows of the soul. While

I'm using this metaphorically, the message is to look around you and notice all the incredible facets of your world.

Enter the beauty of the wind singing through the trees, waterfalls cascading, and brooks rippling. Feel the softness of a flower petal and the sweet song of a sparrow. This world is yours, created for you. You are this world. See it in its purity and as it was created to be. See yourself as the person you were meant to be.

The landscape belongs to the person who looks at it.
~Ralph Waldo Emerson

The real voyage of discovery lies not in finding new lands, but in seeing with new eyes.
~Marcel Proust

sTool 5: Recognition

True reality is always there with you and as you. But your mind's collection of beliefs and thoughts has thrown up a roadblock that prevents you from recognizing it.

As marvelous as our minds' powers to think, believe, and reason are, the real miracle unfolds when our thinking stops. This is where we experience wonder and our deep connection with the Universe. It is from this stance that you want your choices and actions to spring.

Many of us spend our whole lives trying to find ourselves, forgetting the fact that we ARE ourselves.
~Joe Viscomi

A bird doesn't sing because it has an answer; it sings because it has a song.
~Maya Angelou

This is the gift of life for which you were created.

X

Epilogue

When your heart speaks, take good notes.
~Judith Campbell

Your Greatest Gift

You have a gift that only you can give the world—that's the whole reason you're on the planet. Use your precious energy to build a magnificent life that really is attainable. The miracle of your existence calls for celebration every day.
~Oprah Winfrey

The greatest gift you can offer to others and the Universe is you.

We live in a world in which we relate to people in roles as consumer, store clerk, salesperson, patient, computer technician, parent, teacher, and student. In our modern society, this is often necessary for efficiency and the smooth running of social and economic institutions. I am decidedly not advocating that you have deep conversations with everyone you meet throughout the day and week.

We can, however, stay within our greater self as we go about our daily routine. When someone acts out of tune with their soul self and pushes your buttons, you can make the choice to see their real self, and respond from your renewed energy instead of falling back on the old mind frames.

When self-doubts threaten your peace of mind, you can call up one of the many tools you have practiced and regain your authenticity.

When a disappointing event occurs—you didn't get the award, promotion or job—you can accept the disappointment and move on. Drawing upon your reserve of tools to keep you aligned with your greater self, you can quickly banish any thoughts that would keep you from your purpose and happiness.

You have made the shift. Allow yourself to be the person you are.

Each of us was born with wings . . . [and] has the ability to go farther than we ever thought possible, to do things beyond our wildest imaginings.
~Barbara Stanny

Somewhere deep within you
is a song
that plays softly,
always . . .
a song you can hear
only if you're very quiet,
and very still . . .
a song of life,
and dreams, and wisdom . . .
a call to adventure
on a path
that's uniquely yours.
~Author Unknown

Author's Note

Thank you for reading the messages of this book.
I feel deeply blessed to have you as a reader. I hope that in some small way I have contributed to your journey in greatness.

Warmest wishes for your continued happiness and success.
May waves of aloha, joy, and abundance energize your world.

Dr. Jan
Hawaii
November 2011

About the Author

Jan grew up in a log cabin in a small town in the Midwest, USA. There was no electricity or indoor plumbing. She was a shy, sensitive girl who had a big dream to get a college degree and learn how to ease the poverty and injustices that she saw around her.

At age five, when visiting her grandmother in Santa Barbara, she saw the ocean for the first time and fell in love with it. She wondered why everyone couldn't live the life of their dreams surrounded by the natural beauty of nature.

After ten years of working part time as a waitress and typist, getting married and raising four children, she finally fulfilled her first dream of earning a university doctorate.

Her second dream came true when she got a position teaching human development and psychology at the University of Hawaii. Loving challenges and staying fit, at age forty-five she ran her first marathon in the California Redwoods.

A third dream was realized when she set up a private practice in San Francisco specializing in discretionary time use—making your leisure count. Compelled to write on this topic so close to her heart, with the help of her literary agent she was thrilled to have her first book published by the prestigious Wiley and Sons, New York.

Since then she has written eight more books, including *5 Minutes A Day Dream-Action Path*; *Quotes, Questions & Actions for Global Under-standing*; and *The Mighty Power of Your Beliefs—Dream, Believe, Prosper!*

Jan currently lives in an oceanfront home in Hawaii and teaches online university classes in psychology. Her programs, seminars, and lectures have been presented to a wide range of audiences, and through business and professional organizations worldwide. She has a private practice specializing in creative time use and prosperity.

Bibliography

Anderson, Walter Truett. *The Next Enlightenment: Integrating East and West in a New Vision of Human Evolution.* New York: St. Martin's Press, 2003.

Bourne, Edmund J. *Global Shift: How A New Worldview Is Transforming Humanity.* Oakland, CA: New Harbinger/Noetic Books; copublished with the Institute of Noetic Sciences, 2009.

Canfield, Jack, Mark Victor Hansen, Bradley Winch, and Susanna Palomares. *Stories for a Better World.* Deerfield Beach, FL: HCI, 2005.

Chandler, Steve. *Shift Your Mind: Shift the World.* Bandon, OR: Robert D. Reed Publishers, 2010.

Coelho, Paulo. The Alchemist: *A Fable about Following Your Dream.* 2nd ed. New York: HarperCollins, 2006.

Cohen, Andrew. *Evolutionary Enlightenment: A New Path to Spiritual Awakening.* New York: SelectBooks, 2011.

Dooley, Mike. *Infinite Possibilities: The Art of Living Your Dreams.* New York: Atria Books; Hillsboro, OR: Beyond Words, 2010.

Eisler, Riane. *The Power of Partnership: Seven Relationships that Will Change Your Life.* Novato, CA: New World Library, 2002.

Fisher-McGarry, Julie. *Be the Change You Want to See in the World: 365 Things You Can Do for Yourself and Your Planet.* San Francisco: Conari Press, 2006.

Florida, Richard. *The Rise of the Creative Class: And How It's Transforming Work, Leisure, Community, and Everyday Life.* New York: Basic Books, 2002.

Gallagher, Winifred. *Rapt: Attention and the Focused Life.* New York: Penguin, 2009. Kindle edition.

Gault, Jan. *Five Minutes A Day Dream-Action Path: Dream the Life & World You Desire, Then Create It.* Honolulu, HI: Ocean Manor, 2009.

Gault, Jan. *Free Time: Making Your Leisure Count.* Hoboken, NJ: John Wiley & Sons, 1983.

Gault, Jan. *The Mighty Power of Your Beliefs.* Honolulu, HI: Ocean Manor, 2000.

Gault, Jan. *Motivational Messages for Miracle Moments.* Honolulu, HI: Ocean Manor, 2007.

Gault, Jan. *Quotes, Questions & Actions for Global Understanding.* Honolulu, HI: Ocean Manor, 2006.

Gearon, Liam. *The Human Rights Handbook: A Global Perspective for Education.* Staffordshire, England: Trentham Books Limited, 2003.

Gladwell, Malcolm. Blink: *The Power of Thinking Without Thinking.* New York: Back Bay Books, 2007.

Gladwell, Malcolm. *The Tipping Point: How Little Things Can Make a Big Difference.* New York: Back Bay Books, 2002.

Harman, Willis. *Global Mind Change: The Promise of the 21st Century.* San Francisco: Berrett-Koehler Publishers, 1998.

Henderson, Hazel, and Daisaku Ikeda. *Toward an Age of Light: Building a Brighter Future for Our Global Family.* Santa Monica, CA: Middleway Press, 2004.

Holland, Gail Bernice. *A Call For Connection: Solutions for Creating a Whole New Culture.* Novato, CA: New World Library, 1998.

Hubbard, Barbara Marx. *Conscious Evolution: Awakening the Power of Our Social Potential.* Novato, CA: New World Library, 1998.

Hubbard, Barbara Marx. *Emergence: The Shift from Ego to Essence; 10 Steps to the Universal Human.* Charlottesville, VA: Hampton Roads Publishing Company/Walsch Books, 2001.

Joshi, Shashikant. *Attitude Shift: Sanskrit Maxims for Contemporary Life and Leadership.* Bangalore, India: Thinking Hearts, 2011. Kindle edition.

Kumar, Satish. *You Are, Therefore I Am: A Declaration of Dependence.* Totnes, Devon, UK: Green Books, 2002.

Laszlo, Ervin. *You Can Change the World: The Global Citizen's Handbook for Living on Planet Earth.* New York: SelectBooks, 2003.

Law, Joseph. *Living Greatness: A Practical Guide to Living an Enlightened Life.* Chatswood, NSW, Australia: New Holland Publishers, 2011.

Lipton, Bruce H. *Biology of Belief: Unleashing the Power of Consciousness, Matter & Miracles.* Felton, CA: Elite Books/Mountain of Love Productions, 2005.

Milord, Susan. *Hands Around the World: 365 Creative Ways to Encourage Cultural Awareness and Global Respect* (Williamson Kids Can! Series). Charlotte, VT: Williamson Publishing, 2003.

Mitchell, Stephen. *Tao Te Ching: A New English Version.* New York: Harper Perennial, 2009. Kindle edition.

Murphy, Joseph. *The Power of Your Subconscious Mind.* Radford, VA: Wilder Publications, 2010.

Nagler, Michael N. *Is There No Other Way? The Search for a Nonviolent Future.* Berkeley, CA: Berkeley Hills Books, 2001.

Nirmala. *Nothing Personal: Seeing Beyond the Illusion of a Separate Self.* 2nd ed. Sedona, AZ: Endless Satsang Foundation, 2009.

Norton, Michael. *365 Ways to Change the World: How to Make a Difference—One Day at a Time.* New York: Free Press, 2007.

Ogilvy, James A. *Creating Better Futures: Scenario Planning as a Tool for a Better Tomorrow.* Oxford: Clarendon Press, 2005.

Petchesky, Rosalind P. *Global Prescriptions: Gendering Health and Human Rights.* London: Zed Books, 2003.

Priesnitz, Wendy. *Challenging Assumptions in Education.* Toronto: Alternate Press, 2000.

Quinn, Robert E. *Change the World: How Ordinary People Can Accomplish Extraordinary Results.* Hoboken, NJ: Jossey-Bass, 2000.

Schlitz, Marilyn Mandala, Cassandra Vieten, and Tina Amorok. *Living Deeply: The Art and Science of Transformation in Everyday Life.* Oakland, CA: New Harbinger/Noetic Books, 2008.

Seigel, Bernie. *Love, Magic, and Mudpies: Raising Your Kids to Feel Loved, Be Kind, and Make a Difference.* Emmaus, PA: Rodale, 2006.

Shostak, Arthur B., ed. *Viable Utopian Ideas: Shaping a Better World.* Armonk, NY: M. E. Sharpe, 2003.

Strong, Maurice. *Where On Earth Are We Going?* Mason, OH: Texere, 2001.

Thoele, Sue Patton. *Growing Hope: Sowing the Seeds of Positive Change in Your Life and the World.* Newburyport, MA: Red Wheel/Weiser, 2004.

Tolle, Eckhart. *A New Earth: Awakening to Your Life's Purpose.* New York: Penguin, 2008.

Toms, Michael. *At the Leading Edge: New Visions of Science, Spirituality, and Society.* Burdett, NY: Larson Publications, 1991.

Tye, Kenneth. *Global Education: From Thought to Action.* Alexandria, VA: Association for Supervision & Curriculum Development, 1991.

Wallensteen, Peter. *Understanding Conflict Resolution: War, Peace and the Global System.* London: SAGE Publications, 2002.

Walljasper, Jan, and Jon Spayde. *Visionaries: People and Ideas to Change Your Life.* Gabriola Island, BC: New Society Publishers, 2001.

Warfield, Janet Smith. *Shift: Change Your Words, Change Your World.* Las Vegas: Word Sculptures Publishing, 2009.

Wilber, Ken. *The Integral Vision: A Very Short Introduction to the Revolutionary Integral Approach to Life, God, the Universe, and Everything.* Boston: Shambhala Publications, 2007.

Williams, Jessica. *50 Facts That Should Change The World 2.0.* New York, The Disinformation Company, 2007.

Wolman, Richard N. *Thinking with Your Soul: Spiritual Intelligence and Why It Matters.* New York: Harmony Books, 2001.

For information on Jan's seminars, training programs, books, and other products, please contact:

Jan Gault International™
415-367-3513 prosper@drjan.net
http://www.drjan.net

Bulk Purchase Discounts

Books are available at deep quantity discounts with bulk purchase for business, educational, or sales promotional use. For information, please e-mail ocean@drjan.net.

Online Audio/Video Consultations with Dr. Jan Are Currently Available

www.ingramcontent.com/pod-product-compliance
Lightning Source LLC
LaVergne TN
LVHW091155080426
835509LV00006B/698

* 9 7 8 0 9 2 3 6 9 9 4 2 0 *